Democracy's Birth in Ancient Rome

Children's Ancient History Books

BABY PROFESSOR

EDUCATION KIDS

Speedy Publishing LLC
40 E. Main St. #1156
Newark, DE 19711
www.speedypublishing.com

Democracy is a form of government which means 'rule of the people'. The name is derived from the Greek words 'demos' for people and 'kratos' for rule.

Modern democratic governments have representatives elected by the people. The head of the government is either elected by the people or chosen by the legislature based on the legal procedures established by the country.

This form of government started in the 6th century BC in Athens, Greece.

The Roman Democracy

The Athenian leader, Cleisthenes, introduced a system of political reforms known as 'demokratia' or 'rule by the people' in 507 BC.

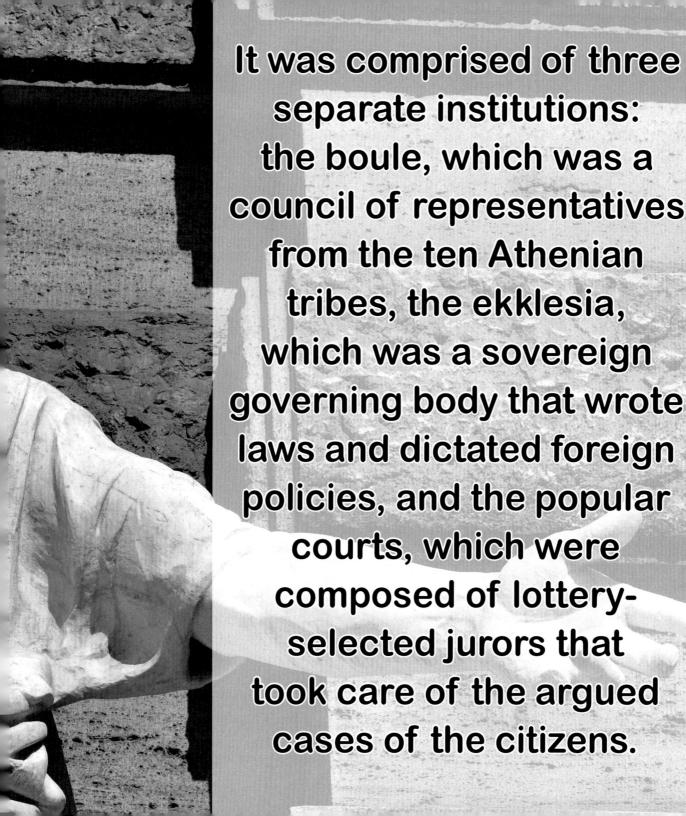

It was comprised of three separate institutions: the boule, which was a council of representatives from the ten Athenian tribes, the ekklesia, which was a sovereign governing body that wrote laws and dictated foreign policies, and the popular courts, which were composed of lottery-selected jurors that took care of the argued cases of the citizens.

Though the Athenian version of democracy survived for only two centuries, Cleisthene's invention was one of the most enduring contributions of Ancient Greece to the modern world.

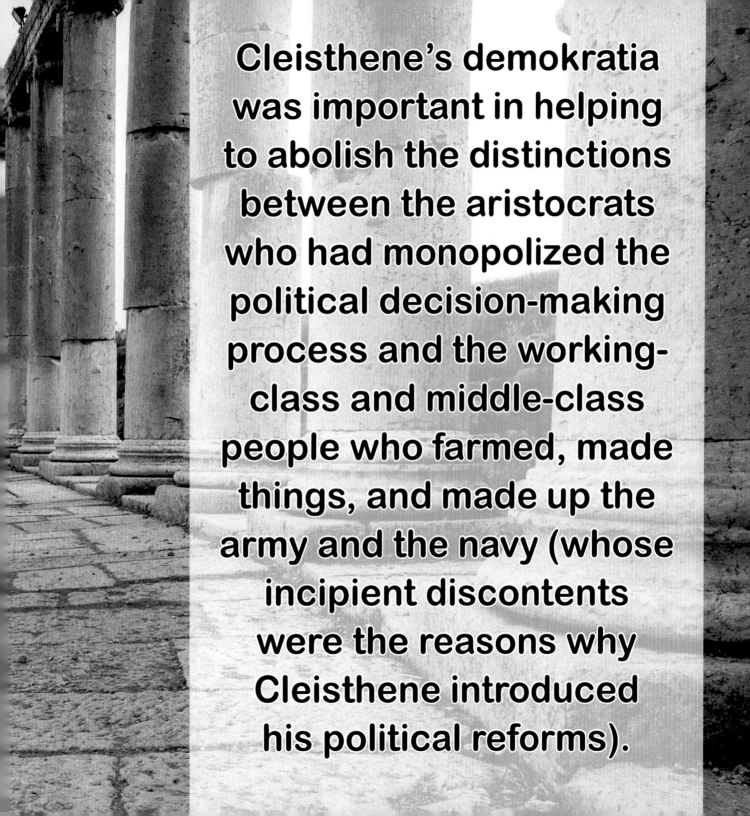

Cleisthene's demokratia was important in helping to abolish the distinctions between the aristocrats who had monopolized the political decision-making process and the working-class and middle-class people who farmed, made things, and made up the army and the navy (whose incipient discontents were the reasons why Cleisthene introduced his political reforms).

However, this equality was limited to a small portion of the Athenian population. Out of all the people, only male citizens who were older than eighteen were part of the demos who could join the democratic process.

The Ekklesia

Any member of the demos was allowed to attend the meeting of the ekklesia. They held 40 meetings per year in a hillside auditorium, the Pnyx, located west of the Acropolis.

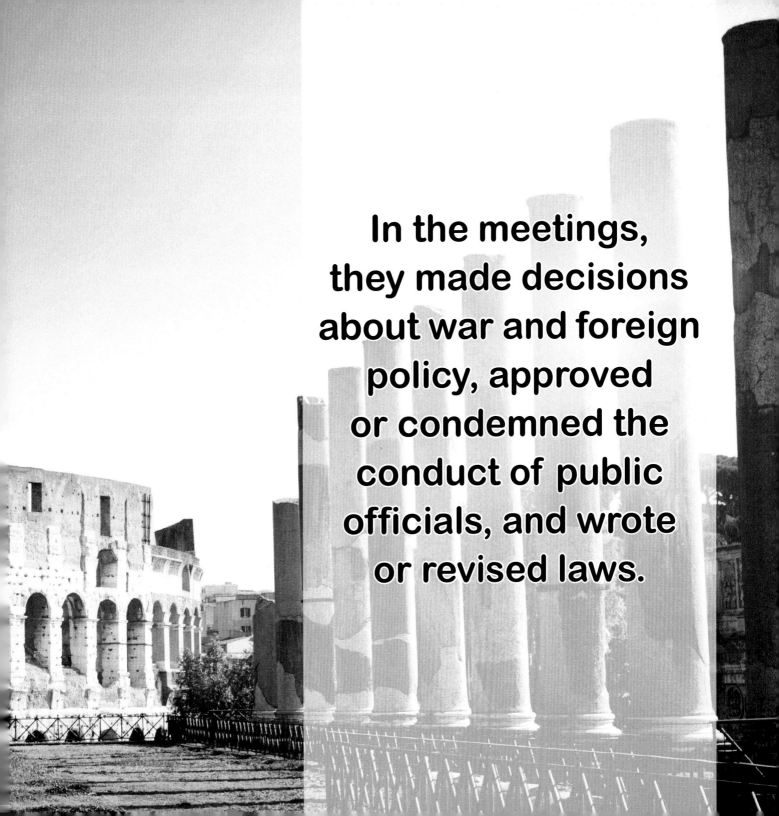

In the meetings, they made decisions about war and foreign policy, approved or condemned the conduct of public officials, and wrote or revised laws.

Among their powers was 'ostracism', by which they could expel a citizen from the Athenian city-state for ten years. The group made their decisions by simple majority vote.

The Boule

This was the Council of Five Hundred, 50 men from each of the ten Athenian tribes. This group met every day and did most of the hands-on work of governing.

The Boule's main function was to decide on matters that came before the ekklesia. Positions in this group were chosen by lot and not by election.

In theory, a lottery was considered more democratic than an election: pure chance could not be influence by things like popularity or money. This lottery system prevented the establishment of a permanent class of civil servants who might use the government to advance or enrich themselves.

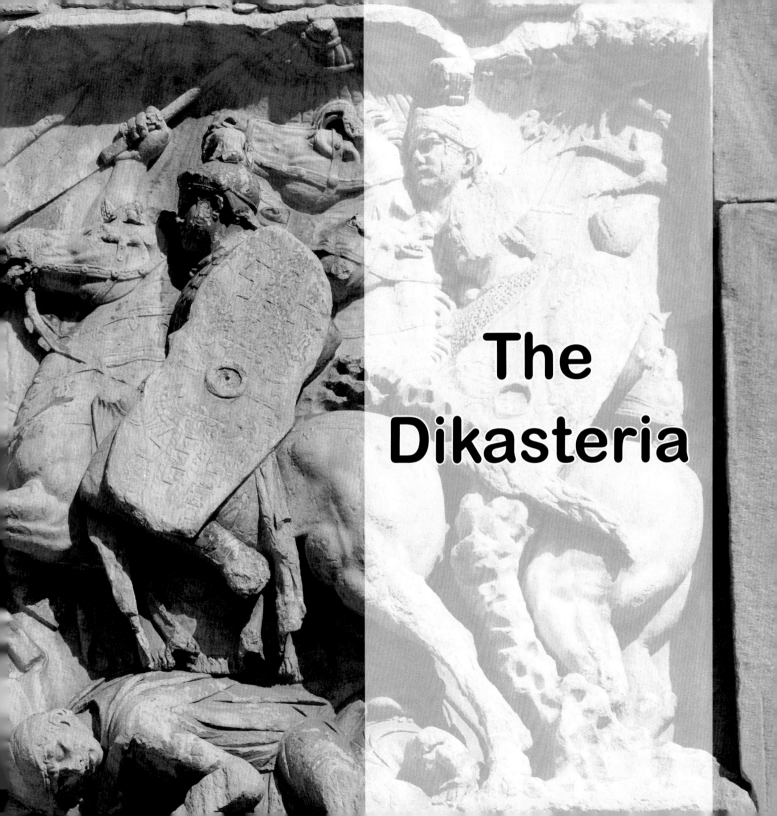

The
Dikasteria

Every day, more than 500 jurors from a pool of male citizens older than 30 were chosen by lot. There were no police in Athens, so the demos themselves brought court cases, argued for the defense or prosecution, and delivered verdicts and sentences majority vote.